KNIGHT PUBLISHING

PORTLAND, OREGON

© Knight Publishing, Inc.
All Rights Reserved
Portland, OR 97219
email: pknight17.1@netzero.net

For my strength, my love, my soul mate; my beautiful and brilliant wife, Rhonda. And to my best friend Ben, the finest jurist I have ever had the honor to work with.

Biography of the Author: Born New Orleans, Louisiana, January 1955. A Veteran of the US Air Force and Air Force Reserve with a BA-Political Science (University of Alaska Anchorage—1988) and Law Degree (University of North Dakota). Currently is a Disability Decision Writer for Administrative Disability Hearings and Appeals (1998—present). Also has written numerous short stories (e.g., Compositions for each of the five Star Trek series. 2000-2004). A trumpet player and composer of Christian hymns as well as Choir Director at St. Matthews Lutheran Church in Anchorage, Alaska and Associate Choir Director at Zion Lutheran Church in Bismarck, North Dakota while attending Law School. Most notable composition "Stand, Praise His Love Eternal" for choir and "Christmas In Ireland" for wind ensemble/concert band. Has been writing since grade school and happily reports "I love to write and I get to do what I love both personally and professionally. Thank you Lord Jesus, I am so blessed."/tm

MAD AS HELL

(AND YOU SHOULD BE TOO)

* * * * *

POLITICS, ECONOMICS, MONEY and the ENVIRONMENT

FOREWORD

Humanity has, until recently, strived to answer the age old questions: Why am I here. What is my purpose in life? I ascribe to that theory that we are here to leave the world a little better than we found it. So far, as we embark on the second decade of the twenty-first century, that task has proven to be more strenuous than ever before.

To paraphrase Sir Winston Churchill: Never before have so few screwed up the world for so many. We are faced with economic and environmental crisis the likes of which no prior civilization has ever seen. We are bombarded by 'spin' and half-truths wrapped in material omissions to the point where we can now be told it is midnight while the midday sun looms overhead.

I also ascribe to another school of thought: A little knowledge can be the catalyst to achieve great things. Hopefully, as you weave your way through this series of short books, you will become enlightened to the dangers confronting us all. Through that enlightenment, it is my sincerest prayer that you will find your resolve and motivation to truly do great things. TM

—I—
OVERVIEW

– I –

As we approach the all important national elections of November 2012, I am compelled to issue this book regarding Politics, Economics, Money (yes it is a different subject from Economics) and the Environment. Before reading this book, it is important to realize that there are certain paradigms which must be remembered:

Change is the only constant in the universe. While humans are resistant to change, we also know that we must be able to identify change and adapt accordingly. Otherwise, we die.

Now is not the time to ask who drained the swamp when you are up to your ass in alligators. In other words, there comes a point in time when knowing who the blame falls in the category of being irrelevant.

Something must be done. So either lead, follow, or get the hell out of my way.

The amount of things I know nothing about is certain. The things I do know about is not certain. However, my desire and resolve to keep learning is Paramount.

It is amazing how many times apples are presented as being oranges and vice versa. More astounding is the lack of objection when the tactic is used to confuse important issues (e.g., abortion and rape; immigration versus being brought into the country as a child, etc.).

In the words of H. L. Mencken[1], "I would have written you a shorter letter, if I had more time."

Of course I know they are lying. Their lips are moving! (They are Politicians)

---

[1] Henry Louis "H. L." Mencken (September 12, 1880 - January 29, 1956), was an American journalist, essayist, magazine editor, satirist, critic of American life and culture, and a scholar of American English.

A bird in the hand is worth more than two in the bush. Actually, it's worth even more than two Bush in the White House.

We <u>ARE</u> all in this together. Will somebody please convince the rich and greedy of that fact.

Behind every Great man is a Great Woman (I know-I married her ☺)

Many scholars believe that mankind will not change for the better until we have hit rock bottom. My question therefore is this: Does bouncing along the bottom meet that definition?

—II—
THE ENVIRONMENT

– II –
The Environment

I have recently been introduced to the music of Nickleback and the song "We've Got To Stay Together." Nowhere in the lyrics is the environment referenced (although the other three main subjects are covered). Love the song. Love the lyrics. But unless they are confident that they can sing under water, I find it necessary to discuss the environment first (because I can't write under water either ☹).

The motivation behind global warming must be explored. Yes, rest assured, there are forces behind the desire to not only continue our growth in global warming, but also to accelerate its impending cataclysmic result. The means through which global warming is expedited are identified with an eye at several of the goals which unknown forces hope to be achieve. To what end those goals are will also be explored with an emphasis on how those changes will impact you and everyone else.

Lastly, positive solutions are explored and calls to action by all to preserve not only ourselves, but also our planet and its diverse life as well, are provided. The list of proffered solutions is not all inclusive. And, this author will gladly recognize other proffered solutions written as part of the book reviews.

As for motivations, the number of theories perhaps could equal the number of stars we see each night (except in Portland, Oregon, where it is cloudy most of the time). For example, the greed of big oil and the Saudi Royals are often cited. Other, more obscure theories would include that the Earth is being terra-formed for aliens on their way to Earth (if they are not already here). Recently, the TV show Fringe proffered the theory that humans from our own future return to our timeline because the screwed up environment they created became even unbearable for them. In the show, the "observers," after taking over the world by use of their telepathic prowess, begin pumping even more carbon monoxide into the atmosphere.

Some economic and political based theories include that a rapid shift to alternative energies is just not feasible (e.g., new generation, distribution and overall logistics in supplying new, alternative energy to the public). One theory no one looks at is that we just don't have the answers to necessary scientific and biological questions to safely produce and distribute new, alternative energy. Scrap that theory! The technologies for green energy exist right now!!!

I think the real motivation is greed with an added impact of reducing the size of the population which has surpassed sustainability. However, from that perspective, the real reason comes to fore. For those of you who have read my novel, "Race Against Global Warming," you too know the real motivation. For those of you who have not read the novel, I'll give you a hint: Control one of life's base necessities and you can control the world.

Having reviewed the possible motivations, let us move on to the projected "end result" if we maintain the status-quo, both in the short-term and long-term: In addition to water shortages, massive droughts and significantly reduced food production, new diseases will emerge from the warmer climate to continue to reduce an already reduced population. Those perpetrating environmental crimes against humanity will have succeeded in opening Pandora's Box. But they will do so without any control.

Humanity may fall completely to the litany of killer events propagated from global warming. Category 5 hurricanes year-round; complete with devastating flooding of Venice, New Orleans, New York, San Francisco, just for starters; massive uncontrollable wildfires; drought 5-times worse than today, worsened by an incredible shortage of water. Food shortages will be unprecedented. No running water, we resort to out-houses.

In 20-years, we, the United States will be just like the poorest towns and cities in India. When these items come to pass, the question of who drained the swamp will be irrelevant.

Make no mistake about it, we are bouncing along the bottom now. If we, as a species, fail to act now, I wouldn't give you a quarter for the last half of your children's lives or a nickel for the lives of any grandchildren. Famine, disease, pestilence, sterility, droughts, new diseases; although I love science-fiction, -—sadly, none of the above potential outcomes are fiction—they will come to pass. Therefore, the real question is: "Are we out of time?"

People complain now that their water bills are climbing at an alarming rate. Rest assured, your complaints are being ignored. Imagine in 20-years paying $10.00 for one gallon of water. One gallon. How could farmers irrigate their crops? The answer, only those few select mega-company farms answerable only to the 1% rich and greedy will have the ability to pay for and receive adequate water supplies.

And surely, no one is going to spend $10.00 just to flush their toilets. New in-home water redistribution systems need to be made so that dishwater, shower water and cooking (spaghetti) water can all be funneled into our toilets. Otherwise, it's Slum-Dog Millionaire Out-House diving for those who keep their heads buried in the sand. And it is my sincerest hope that this book gets a lot of reading in India, because they have been the *beta-test* subjects for Armageddon, as planned for by the rich and greedy, since 1980.

Now if we are not yet out of time, what solutions are available to us? Make no mistake about it, we are at war. A war between the 1% extremely rich and powerful and the 99% of us trying to survive on the meager scraps we find.

We, the 99% need to get educated, dedicated and organized. We must do more than just complain. We must know the solutions available to us and use the ballot box so that no more computerized elections are stolen right out from under our noses. Then we will need to mobilize our insurmountable numbers in peaceful boycotts, through our own established underground economy, through our own ingenuity, build our own hydrogen cars, take ourselves off the electric grid with wind and solar and hydropower (put a water wheel in your back yard).

Stop using banks. Hell, stop using money as much as you can. Set up our own bartering network. Lastly, clean out those unscrupulous few among us who find it easier to steal from us than from the rich and powerful.

Collectively, we can effect peaceful change, while, to paraphrase Harry Truman, we carry our own big stick based on our collective numbers. Remember this constant: There is power in numbers!

—III—
POLITICS

– III –
POLITICS

When Karl Marx declared "religion is the opiate of the masses," he achieved 2 objectives: (1) He caused people to question their own values. (2) He made "politics" more important than even religion.

The once rich orthodox history of the Russian people was the first obstacle abolished under the new Socialist communist regime. Without religion, faith falters, hope fades. Without hope, the people perish.

However, religion should be personal, not corporate. Candidates for the 1% are easily portraying themselves as "the religious, God fearing right." Let me tell you the truth. Those who really believe do not need to pronounce to the world that they are believers. The real faithful practice compassion, love for one another, a sense of community and strong civic duty. The real faithful do so quietly, by example.

The second obstacle eliminated by the communist was to take complete control of the media. In today's controlled media – apples & oranges are freely mixed to confuse the masses: Abortion is murder; Rape victims are sluts. Gays and Lesbians are abominations. And despite an already overburdened foster child systems, birth of rape-produced offspring is advocated. More children, greater poverty.

Women who rightfully seek control over their reproduction choices are freely chastised by the alleged pro-life; right wing; highly religious but really highly hypocrite 1% rich and greedy. The rich and greedy control the media and readily confuse the issues: What used to be the "hot button issue" of "Gays in the military," has been replaced with "Same Sex Marriage" Opposition. Other hot topic issues promulgated by the 1% rich and greedy: Immigration, the Deficit, Terrorism, Abortion, and "Beware the Creeping Socialism." (I'm saving "trickle down" for the Economics section).

Now for those of you have been alive long enough to vote in at least four Presidential Elections: Haven't you heard the above issues every four years? The answer should be a resounding "Yes." And after the election, what gets done about these allegedly important issues? Absolutely nothing!

Nothing is done because these are not the real issues. The real issues are jobs, taxes, food supply, water supply, energy, infrastructure, and last but definitely not least, education. Let's take the newest issue: "Same Sex Marriage." Here's reality, the Constitution requires <u>Equal Protection of the Law</u>. Your liberties end where your neighbor's nose begins. Democratic Government has absolutely no business promulgating laws impacting personal choice—period. And remember the old adage of denied constitutional protections in pre-WWII Germany. First they came for my neighbor, and I said nothing. Next they came for my Rabbi, and I remained silent. Finally, they came for me and I could not be heard over the sound of gunfire used to kill me.

Equal Protection of the Law means just that. Women have control over their own bodies and reproductive choices; and people get to marry who they love (let me know if you've heard these words before), regardless of age (sorry, adults only), race, sex, religion, ethnicity or political affiliation (these words are in Congressional statutes derived from the U.S. Constitution, The Bill of

Rights, and *starry decisis* (i.e., case precedence from the U.S. Supreme Court).

But the rich and greedy have gotten 49% of the 98% to buy into their confusing of the issues. So in reality, we (half of the 98%) have done great damage to our democracy by preventing Equal Protection of the Law.

(Okay, now to assure you that the math does add up: We are really 98% plus 1% of the rich and greedy and 1% of dishonest people thinking they can get rich off the poor by helping the rich and greedy in their *spin and control of the media.*)

Ahh, the right wing conservatives. They seek to control everything. Your religion, your beliefs, your very existence! So every 2 years, they parade out the same oranges & tell you they are apples: Abortion, Immigration, Gays in the Military, Same Sex Marriage, Prayer in Schools, Patriotism, and yes, even Taxes. All the while, lying better than a Turkish rug on a hardwood floor.

Intellectually, the game they play has a name. It's called M-I-S-D-I-R-E-C-T-I-O-N. A con artist would call it the old shell game. Bottom line: They've got you focusing on the wrong things. And it is all done through Politics: How to get the masses to give them the authority and power to shaft us, and take away our life, liberty and property.

From 2000 to 2008, we've lost liberty, freedom, jobs, rights and faith. Two Towers, two wars, a 12 trillion dollar debt that Congress did not see in submitted budgets, two stolen elections, and war crimes by us that will never see the light of day.

Now we have the Patriot Act; Big Brother everywhere, veterans with little if any benefits; union busting; jobs shipped overseas; skyrocketing gasoline, water and food prices climbing while packaging and portions shrink, new strains of flesh eating & other diseases, and one fourth of Antarctica melting into the sea in a couple of months after the rich and greedy elitist hired scientist said it would take 20-years.

Now there are many among us who, rightfully so, say that our political process is broken. However, if you are part of the 1%, you'd say the political system is just right. You've got the elections computerized and you've got the Electoral College.

If I were in an auditorium with 5,000 plus in the attendance, and asked for a show of hands for those who believe candidates for President are elected by the majority of ballots cast, I dread the thought of seeing almost 5,000 hands go up. All wrong. It's the Electoral college.

And the elite have convinced the population that there are "battleground" states. Polling numbers allegedly too close to call. This year, Wisconsin and Pennsylvania joined the list of the so-called "battleground states," such as Florida, Ohio, New Mexico, and Colorado.

If the "Republicans" steal this election (again, through either Ohio or Florida, or worse, Pennsylvania), they will only need 2 battleground states to do it. No problem, it will only require the push of a button thanks to computerized elections which the results cannot be verified or challenged.

We need a super-Pac the likes of which has never been seen before: Service organizations; all Unions; all real religious churches (Jewish, Catholic, Lutherans, Methodist, Presbyterians, and American Baptist), NOW (The National Organization of Women); the ACLU: the VFW; the American Legion; DAV (Disabled American Veterans); the AFL-CIO; the Teamsters; the Jewish Anti-Defamation League; the Knights of Columbus, the National Federation of Teachers, just to name a few.

And of course, I haven't even touched on what the real issues are that politics never wants you to think about. Things that your taxes never go to: Jobs; Education; Food; Energy; Healthcare; Infrastructure; & Social Security. Worse I cannot even begin to list the lost opportunities for all Americans to have a legitimate shot at the American Dream. Twenty five percent of home purchases since 2000 are now in foreclosure. Twenty-Five percent of good paying jobs shipped overseas. Twenty five percent of high school Graduates cannot afford College. Twenty five percent young Americans traumatized by violence, drugs, and worse. Thousands of young American men and women killed or permanently maimed in mind and body after serving multiple tours in Iraq and Afghanistan.

Today the one percent has succeeded in destroying twenty five percent of the 99% in only 10 years. Their ultimate goal is to make it 50% by 2020. So the real question you need to ask yourself is this: "Do you want to be part of that 50%? Read this book and give it to your friends and you won't be.

The Lie of "Creeping Socialism"

At its height, communist regimes, under the guise of a Socialist Party, had an average of 40% of the population tied up as national government/party workers, plus another average of 20% of the population in the military. Consequently, nothing was being produced. Food was scarce and costly when you could find it. All farms were co-opted into the national distribution system which in and of itself, was worse than you'd find in most third world countries. Taxation averaged 25% for the lower two-thirds of earned income citizens while party members and bureaucrats paid little if any while enjoying the best of everything. Sounds vaguely familiar yet drastically different from what we have in America today. By the way, communist regimes survived only 70-to-75 years and their collapse was both surprising and quick.

In America, under the administrations of Truman, Johnson and Clinton, the size of the national government work force was never higher than 15%. The military never surpassed 10%. Today, the federal government work force is at 9.8% and the military is down to 8%. This portion of the population roughly represents 15% of the country's middle class, paying an average of 15% federal taxes and 8% state taxes. They are among the top 15% of educated Americans, possessing a 4 year or higher degree. Almost 20% of the federal government work force has an advanced degree, such as a jurist doctorate, masters degree or doctorate in medicine, biology, meteorology, or mechanical/electrical/hydrology/aeronautical engineering. And they all vote.

Collectively, the federal government workforce and military pays over one-third of the country's revenue in taxes; supports colleges and universities with tuition and alumni funds; supports their local churches and schools. In turn , they administer complex laws governing water rights, food safety, drug safety, community health, consumer safety, energy (including hydropower dams) and nuclear power generation, transportation logistics and safety (including highway, rail, airline and marine distribution), education federal funding, Medicare and Social Security, just to name but a portion of all the jobs federal civilian and military personnel perform in the name of peace and in protecting communities. And they perform their duties with passion, with dedication and with honor.

As can be discerned from above. To apply the lie that America is on a path of "creeping socialism" is but another of the multitude of bald faced lies perpetrated by the rich and greedy few. Thanks to the lies of the rich and greedy, our federal civilian and military workers are being portrayed daily as the "bad guys." Why? Well the answer is fairly obvious. They want our taxes to pay for their government contracts and subsidies (example: Exxon averaged $400 billion dollars every three months in profits. That's 1.2 billion dollars a year, while gouging the American people at the pump. But, by an almost unanimous vote in the House in 2011, $368 million dollars was <u>given</u> to the oil companies for research and development; plus over $600 million dollars given to General Electric. Instead, Congress holds hearing on one failed Solar Panel Company for a loan of less than half a million dollars).

The rich and greedy don't want to see Medicare, Medicaid and Social Security to continue, despite the fact that we taxpayers (the 98%) have already paid for those program in payroll deductions five-times over since 1950.

The G. W. Bush Administration ran the Iraq and Afghanistan Wars "off the books" for 10-years. Under the Patriot Act, all Congress was allowed to do was merely give its consent to the President to go to war. No budgets were submitted, no bills of appropriation were drawn up, basically the administration had a blank check. Despite this obvious circumvention of the U.S. Constitution, if there were legal challenges to what the administration was doing, they were all effectively squelched or crushed. The end result, over 5,000 young men and women dead from military combat. Countless more (25,000 to 40,000) wounded mentally, physically or both. In-turn, the Bush administration passed new GI-Bills limiting educational opportunities for veterans and limiting medical care for veterans.

My blood pressure almost came through the top of my skull as I stood in a VA Hospital hallway reading a poster that read: "If you served in Iraq or Afghanistan, and suffered a combat related injury, you <u>may</u> be eligible for up to 2 years VA medical care." That's not what enlistees signed up for at the time of the their enlistments. But, of course, without the Constitution, there was no need for the administration to worry about the illegality of ex post facto laws (i.e., laws written after the fact).

Federal employees and military pay taxes and buy goods and services which, in-turn, stimulates the economy and really does create more jobs. They provide necessary and vital services everyday to the American people. They are not the bad guys. We are no more headed towards Socialism than I am headed to the moon without a spacesuit. It is all a lie with the sole purpose to take your hard earned money and give you squat in return.

Oh yes, in case you are wondering how the money was gathered and used for the war efforts, it was truly borrowed and stolen. The administration raided the Social Security Administration Trust Fund, the Federal Employees Retirement Trust Fund and kicked 35% to 50% of potential military retirees out within months of their retirement while stealing from that Trust Fund earmarked by Congress years ago. That accounted for one-third of the war spending, mostly up front, about 3 Trillion dollars. The rest, borrowed on Treasury and government bonds, totaling about 6 Trillion dollars.

So ask yourself these two questions: How do you spend 9 Trillion dollars on wars where the troops are in Hummers that bullets can penetrate like sticking your finger through wet toilet paper?

—IV—
ECONOMICS

-IV-
ECONOMICS

The thread that binds us all: Economics. Thanks to the likes of the Koch brothers; Rupert Murdoch and other super greedy, super rich; Economics is the thread that has been unraveling like a cheap suit. The scary part is that the unraveling is entirely by design.

I've seen where 25% of our jobs that paid a descent wage, have been transferred overseas. In – turn, unemployment in 10 years, has hit 25%. Don't be fooled by the bogus unemployment numbers put out every quarter. We've lost over 40 million jobs from 2002 to 2010 (roughly 5 million jobs a year). The so called official numbers do not count those unemployed who are no longer eligible for unemployment. Those numbers do not count the number of spouses who previously did not have to work, but are now forced to look for work because the breadwinner's job disappeared, often without any warning. Those numbers also do not include the millions stuck in low-wage, part-time jobs, without any vacation, heath or retirement benefits.

All the achievements from unions & solidarity built over 50 years from 1940 to 1990 have been decimated by the greedy rich. What's worse, the greedy rich are still not satisfied. They want that 25% to grow into 99%. Those greedy rich really do want to return to the dark ages. The days of Kings and Queens.

Of course, it all starts with eliminating jobs while continuing to tax: Federal & State exercise taxes on necessities: Gasoline, Telephone, Electricity, Natural Gas, Cable TV and Water, Sewer rates and Garbage. They (Congress) spend our tax money for the rich and greedy defense contracts, oil company research gifts, and only the Almighty knows what else they spend our hard earned tax dollars for. Their expenditures are exceeding 3-Trillion a year and our taxes only cover half that amount. Yet they balk at paying their fair share of taxes and complain that the debt ceiling is too high (But they caused the debt in the first place !).

And while that nasty 1% of greedy rich are destroying your life and dreams, they steal your retirement by manipulating the money markets. They scheme to make your "golden" years a nightmare by eradicating the safety nets of Social Security and Medicaid.

All the while, the rich and greedy play "war" using our sons and daughters as cannon fodder. Leaving Veterans and their families in the cold. Leaving families devastated in lost jobs, foreclosed homes and broken dreams.

If you are not boiling and enraged at this point, call the morgue, you must be dead.

—V—
MONEY

-V-
MONEY

There was once a time when every dollar printed was backed by silver and gold. There were no national banks. Community Savings & Loans were the majority, local money in local hands. For over 100 years the United States Government ran quite well without a federal Income Tax, until 1913.

If you kept track of all the taxes your really pay, you'd find that one-fourth of your gross income is eaten up by taxes every year. But our roads crumble, bridges collapse, colleges raise tuition, doctors charge more, food cost more, fuel cost more, and some of our 98% are swindled out of their homes by banks presenting variable mortgages as fixed, or giving equity variable mortgages as fixed.

Now I'm not even going to touch upon the argument that the Income Tax is illegal and unenforceable. As a Law School graduate, I can tell you the only three letters in the alphabet that I fear are "I-R-S." I take the basic deductions and see 25% of my income disappear into the great beyond. Realistically, I'm thankful to the Almighty that I've got a job, and I prayed for a decent living, adding that I would not be greedy. My prayers are answered daily and I quietly pay unto Caesar what is Caesar's.

Instead, I look at taxes as a necessary evil, no different than us saving money by paying ourselves first. One political party (you really must call up Harry Truman's 1948 Convention Acceptance Speech and listen to it) points out that our debt is growing exponentially and we must get it under control. What they don't tell you is that they are the ones who caused the debt, since day one through to the present time. All the while protecting the rich by signing a Pledge Not To Tax The Rich, drawn up by Mr. Grover Norquist.

The politicians say they are blackmailed to do the bidding of the rich because the list of those pledging not to tax the rich and greedy will be made public. I say "We The People" make the list public. Once we know who they are, maybe we can put them on a Camel and pass them through the eye of a needle ☺.

And, now that they've tapped out all the Trust funds,

where can the rich and greedy steal from next? Why from everyone else's retirement funds! You put your money in an IRA, Roth or 401-K or TSP retirement plan. All retirement plans put your money into the Stock Market. We know the Market can and often is manipulated. In October 2008, as the rich and greedy started a selling spree, we lost significant amounts in our retirement funds, to the tune of 30% (wow, that's even more than we pay in taxes. Add it together: The middle class pays 25% in excise and annual income taxes, and the money controllers have let the rich and greedy steal 30% more of our money—AND THEY WILL CONTINUE TO DO IT EVERY YEAR—so in reality, the middle class is paying 55% of its income to the rich and greedy).

You can expect such black Monday Market events to happen with more regularity, as often as three to four times a year. Because the frequency will increase to such regularity, the rich and greedy even managed to remove protections provided to members of Congress when they used "insider information (the same thing Martha Stewart was sent to prison for)." Now they too will get 30% stolen from their retirements as well ☺

As savers, we, who have to work, have no time to play the Market like the rich and greedy, so our money remains at their mercy and their paid manipulators. Now do you recognize who the bad guys really are?

Bottom-line is this: If you can save anything at all of your hard cold cash, that may be enough to keeps you from complete financial devastation. Remember the old adage of a bird in the hand? It is true. If you saved a dollar a day, you have $365.00 in the bank at the end of the year (Whoopee ☹). Now you know why a 1½% cost-of-living increase means nothing to 98% of the population while the 2% politicians and greedy rich see mega buck increases.

Okay, so you've got to do better that a dollar a day. So if you save $25 a paycheck, that's $50 a month and by the end of the year, you've got $600—DON'T TOUCH IT—open a credit union account (stay away from banks). Next year shoot for a thousand dollars at the end of the year.

My wife and I only claim 1 exemption, so we know we're getting a refund. We took our refunds and stuck them in a safety deposit box and called it our new car fund. After four years, we got a new car. We also have a saying: If you can't pay cash for it—YOU DON'T REALLY NEED IT !!!!!!!!!! Credit only makes the rich and greedy richer and greedier.

And, of course, PAY YOURSELF FIRST. Put money into savings before you start thinking about a new cell phone and contract (We have a prepaid with rollover for emergencies. No text, no internet, just emergencies. We spend $10 a year to keep it active). Also, Do Your Homework. There are better prices, often for even better products. You have to take responsibility for your own money. Otherwise, you're a fool. And everyone knows that old adage: A fool and his money are soon parted. Don't get greedy. And if it sounds too good to be true, it's because it is.

The rich 1% controls 98% of the wealth—AND THEY WANT IT ALL !!!!!!!!!!!!!!!!!!! If the rich paid 25% in taxes like the 98% of us, we would have a surplus that would be the envy of the world. Social Security and Medicaid would be miniscule expenses if everyone paid their fair share. And the real crazy part is this: All that money—it is only paper. Nothing is backing it up. It's all Monopoly money to the rich. The Federal Reserve is only incorporated to control the paper money supply so we don't have runaway inflation like pre-WWII Germany.

And for those of you fortunate enough to be near retirement, investigate this advice: When you go to get an annuity, the plan holder will forcefully recommend a lifetime annuity. The only problems with that option are: (1) It is computed out to age 104, with the last year consisting of a few thousand dollars. (2) It leaves your money in their hands and under their control. They keep sticking it in the Stock Market so the rich and greedy can pull out chunks of it on Black Mondays.

As for me, I'm taking a 15-year annuity, pulling out 100% of my funds, dedicating all of it to me, in an iron-clad 15-year payout contract. Sure, we'll have more than we'll need monthly. But we will save 25% a year to cover the next 10-years, along with our Social Security (assuming it is still around). We'll save 12% of a year over the second 10-years for the unlikely event that I live to be 100 and my wife lives to be 94. We control our own hard earned cold cash when we retire. Not the brokers.

Don't believe their stories about 10% to 50% earnings on your retirement. Those days are long dead and gone. Hopefully, if the government ever gets straightened onto the path it used to be on in the 40's and 50's, investors will again realize significant interest gains. But I don't expect to see that for another 10-to-15 years, and that's if we're fortunate to stop the overthrow of our democracy by the rich and greedy 1% aristocrats.

Once "We The People" stand together and say we want an ounce of gold for our performed services and created goods, then we begin to regain the power lost. We, the 98%, must restore our **solidarity**, we must control our food and water supplies and cost, we must stand up and stand together because we truly are all in this together. And it all starts with us, together, the 98%, fighting the Political, Economic, Money, Environment poisoning rich and greedy.

As the foreword of this book reflects: With a little bit of knowledge, you can do great things. I'll stand with you, just let me know when you're ready to take back your country and constitution at the polls and through community involvement. Until that time, I remain your most veracious advocate. Thomas Martin.

www.ingramcontent.com/pod-product-compliance
Lightning Source LLC
Chambersburg PA
CBHW061521180526
45171CB00001B/272